Introduction to Sequenced Collections in Java 21

by

Deepak Vohra

Foreword

The Collections Framework in Java forms the basis for representing data structures and algorithms. The collections framework provides types for collections of objects - sets, maps, lists, etc. Sequenced collections in Java 21 refurbish the collections framework by adding the notion of sequence in elements of a collection. Sequenced collections provide an encounter order to elements of a collection. Sequenced collections are implemented pervasively in the collections framework.

What This Book Covers?

The book introduces sequenced collections as a new language feature in Java 21.

What You Need for This Book?

The book requires some knowledge of the collections framework in Java.

Who is This Book For?

The primary target audience of the book is Java developers.

Table Of Contents

1 Introduction

In this chapter, we will cover the following topics:

- What is a Sequenced Collection
- How to Use a Sequenced Collection from JavaScript
- Common Uses of Sequenced Collections

The Java Collections framework defines a collection as a group of objects, called elements of the collection. The root interface in a collection hierarchy is `java.util.Collection`. Other classes and interfaces for commonly used data structures such as a list, set, and map are defined within the collection hierarchy. Some collections are ordered, and others are unordered. Before the new language feature – sequenced collections - the only interface/class that has some notion of a "sequence" is the `java.util.AbstractSequentialList` interface.

1.1 What is a Sequenced Collection

A sequenced collection is a collection that consists of elements, or entries, in a well-defined sequence in terms of first element, second element.... last element. "Ordering" of elements does not imply a natural ordering of the element values, such as 1,2,3 …, or a,b,c…., but the sequenced element values could have natural ordering if so defined in a collection. The sequenced elements may be accessed using "sequential access" in contrast to accessing a collection's elements with "random access", such as with an index position. In a sequenced collection, each element other than the first and last elements has a successor and a predecessor. The first element has only a successor, and the last element has only a predecessor. An iterator defined on a sequenced collection has the notion of direction. An iterator could traverse a sequenced collection in the forward direction; from first element to last element. Or, an iterator could traverse a sequenced collection in the reverse direction from the last to the first element. The main features of a sequenced collection are: adjacency, double-ended ness, navigability, and forward/reverse iteration.

1.2 How to Use a Sequenced Collection from JavaScript

The reference types provided by Java including the new reference types for sequenced collections can be accessed from client-side JavaScript using the `Java.type()` method. As an example, an object of type can be instantiated using the new operator as follows:

```
var anArrayList = new
Java.type("java.util.ArrayList");
```

1.3 Common Uses of Sequenced Collections

Sequenced collections have several uses, some of which are:

1.3.1 Graph Search

A Graph data structure consists of nodes/vertices and edges connecting the nodes. A graph has adjacency built into it - some nodes are adjacent while other nodes may have intermediate nodes between them.   Graph traversal order is significant in graph search when traversing from one vertex/node to another. In graph search, a graph search algorithm could be unidirectional, implying only directed in one direction. Or graph search could be bi-directional, implying a search in both the forward and reverse directions.

1.3.2 Decision Tree Model

A decision tree model consists of a sequence of queries in which the outcome from one query determines the next query. Boosted decision trees is a type of machine learning technique that makes use of sequential development. The Boosting technique produces a sequence of classifiers starting with weak classifiers that develop into strong classifiers. Each decision tree in Boosting depends on the preceding decision tree/s.

1.3.3 Hierarchical Packaging

Hierarchical packaging requires that the directories/folders be created and accessed in an ordered sequence. As a simple example, the class `java.util.LinkedHashSet` consists of the class `LinkedHashSet` in the package `java.util`. When importing, or using the class, the fully qualified name of the class must declare the package and the class in an ordered sequence; first "java", second "util", and third "LinkedHashSet"

1.4 Summary

In this chapter we defined a sequenced collection, and listed its uses. We also discussed how a collections framework type could be used in JavaScript.

In the next chapter we explore the collections framework's support for sequences before the new language feature - sequenced collections.

2 Before Sequenced Collections

Doesn't the Java Collection Framework already have several types that provide sequence to a collection? In this chapter, we will cover the limited scope of sequences before the new language feature.

The `java.util.List` interface is defined as "An ordered collection (also known as a sequence)." The following are the methods from the `List` interface that have support for sequencing and ordering.

Table 2.1. Methods in List

Method Name	Description	Support for Sequences
iterator()	Returns an iterator over the elements in this list represented by an Iterator<E> object.	The elements are in proper sequence as they appear in the list.
listIterator()	Returns an iterator over the elements in this list represented by a ListIterator<E> object.	The elements are in proper sequence as they appear in the list.
listIterator(int index)	Same as the listIterator() method but the iterator starts at the specified position in the list.	The elements are in proper sequence starting at the specified position.
toArray() toArray(T[] a)	Returns an array that contains all the elements in the list from the first element to the last element.	The elements in the array returned are in proper sequence as they appear in the list.

The `java.util.Deque<E>` interface represents a double-ended queue that supports adding and removing elements at both ends. The `Deque` interface provides the following methods to support ordering and sequences.

Table 2.2. Methods in Deque

Method Name	Description	Support for Sequences

addFirst(E e)	Adds an element to the front of the deque if possible, or throws an exception.	Adds specified element as the new first element.
addLast(E e)	Adds an element to the end of the deque if possible, or throws an exception.	Adds specified element as the new last element.
descendingIterator()	Returns a descending iterator over the elements in the deque.	The elements are returned in reverse sequential order.
getFirst()	Gets the first element in the deque.	The element is not removed and continues to be the first element.
getLast()	Gets the last element in the deque.	The element is not removed and continues to be the last element.
iterator()	Returns a forward iterator over the elements in the deque.	The elements are returned in proper sequential order as they appear in the deque.
offerFirst(E e)	Adds an element at the front of the deque, capacity permitting.	The added element becomes the new first element in the deque.
offerLast(E e)	Adds an element at the end of the deque, capacity permitting.	The added element becomes the new last element in the deque.
pollFirst()	Polls the first element and returns and removes it unless the deque is empty. Returns null if the deque is empty.	The second element in the deque becomes the new first element, if the deque has a second element.
pollLast()	Polls the last element and returns and removes it unless the deque is empty. Returns null if the deque is empty.	The second to last element in the deque becomes the new last element, if the deque has a second to last element.

removeFirst()	Removes the first element and returns its value unless the deque is empty. Returns an exception if the deque is empty.	The second element in the deque becomes the new first element, if the deque has a second element.
removeLast()	Removes the last element and returns its value unless the deque is empty. Returns an exception if the deque is empty.	The second to last element in the deque becomes the new last element, if the deque has a second to last element.

The `java.util.ListIterator` is able to traverse a list in forward, or reverse direction. The interface provides the following methods for iteration in either direction.

Table 2.3. Methods in ListIterator

Method Name	Description
hasNext()	Finds if the list has an element in the forward direction. Returns true/false.
next()	Returns the next element by traversing the list in the forward direction.
hasPrevious()	Finds if the list has an element in the reverse direction. Returns true/false.
previous()	Returns the previous element by traversing the list in the reverse direction.

The `java.util.NavigableSet<E>` interface provides bi-directional navigation (ascending or descending) within a set. It provides the following navigation-related methods that preserve ordering.

Figure 2.4. Methods in NavigableSet

Method Name	Description
iterator()	Returns an iterator over the elements in the set in ascending order.
descendingIterator()	Returns an iterator over the elements in the set in descending order.
descendingSet()	Returns a reverse order view of the NavigableSet.

The `java.util.NavigableMap<E>` interface provides bi-directional navigation (ascending or descending key order) within a map. It provides the following navigation-related methods that preserve ordering.

Table 2.5. Methods in NavigableMap

Method Name	Description
descendingMap()	Returns a NavigableMap<K,V> object with a reverse order view of the mappings.
descendingKeySet()	Returns a NavigableSet<K> with a reverse order view of the keys in the map.
navigableKeySet()	Returns a NavigableSet<K> with a forward order view of the keys in the map.
firstEntry()	Returns the first key/value entry in the map. The least key determines the first entry. Returns null if map is empty.
lastEntry()	Returns the last key/value entry in the map. The greatest key determines the last entry. Returns null if map is empty.
pollFirstEntry()	Polls the first key/value entry in the map. The least key determines the first entry. Returns the first entry, and also removes the entry from the map. The mapping associated with the second least key becomes the new first entry. Returns null if map is empty.
pollLastEntry()	Polls the last key/value entry in the map. The greatest key determines the last entry. Returns the last entry, and also

	removes the entry from the map. The mapping associated with the second greatest key becomes the new last entry. Returns null if map is empty.

2.2 Summary

In this chapter we explored the types in the collections framework that provide a limited scope for sequences even before the new language feature of sequenced collections.

In the next chapter we explore what is new in the sequenced collections language feature.

3 What is New in Sequenced Collections

In this chapter, we will cover what is new in the sequenced collections language feature.

As discussed in Chapter 2, the Java Collections framework already has limited support for ordered and sequenced collections in several of its types. Java 21 improves on the support for sequenced collections as follows:

- It adds three new collection types to represent sequenced collections. The new types include some new methods with default implementations, and some methods promoted from existing types, some with added default implementation.
- It rearranges the Collections framework type hierarchy to include the new types.
- It makes support for sequenced collections uniform across the Collections framework, including special semantics for specific types if necessary.

Next, we shall discuss each of the new collection types in some detail.

3.1 New Collection Types

The new types are the interfaces SequencedCollection<E>, SequencedSet<E>, and SequencedMap<K,V>. In the new type hierarchy the SequencedCollection<E> is a subtype of Collection as shown in Figure 3.1. SequencedCollection<E> extends the Collection<E>, and Iterable<E> interfaces. The new collection types are shown in a different font in the subsequent diagrams.

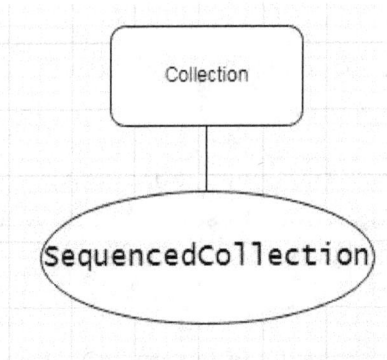

Figure 3.1. New type SequencedCollection

The SequencedCollection<E> type has the following characteristics:

- The elements in a sequenced collection have a well-defined encounter order
- Supports operations at both ends
- Is reversible

Encounter order implies that the elements have a linear arrangement starting with a first element, followed by successor elements, and finally the last element. The elements keep their adjacency within the collection with a predecessor/successor hierarchy. The SequencedCollection<E> type defines the following new method.

Table 3.1. New Methods in SequencedCollection

Method Name and Return type	Description
SequencedCollection<E> reversed()	Returns a reverse ordered view of the collection.

The new reversed() method is in fact renamed/promoted from the NavigableSet::descendingSet method.

The SequencedCollection<E> type promotes the following methods, which we discussed in Chapter 2, from the Deque interface; the add* and remove* methods are optional:

- addFirst(E)
- addLast(E)
- getFirst()
- getLast()
- removeFirst()
- removeLast()

Essentially the SequencedCollection<E> type is a rehash of existing API with one new method. The emphasis in sequenced collections is to make support for sequenced operations uniform within the Collections framework with a few new methods while keeping some methods/operations optional. What an "optional operation" means is that if a collection implementation does not support the operation the UnsupportedOperationException is thrown.

The SequencedCollection<E> type makes the List and Deque types as its subtypes, and adds a new type called SequencedSet<E> as shown in Figure 3.2.

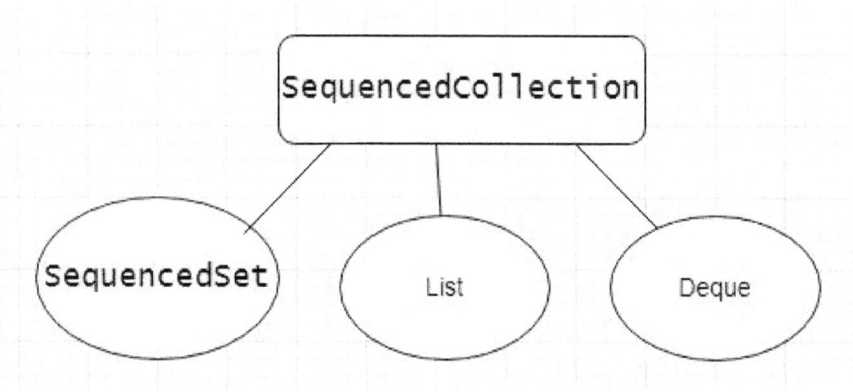

Figure 3.2. SequencedCollection subtypes

13

All super-interfaces of SequencedSet in Java 21 are Collection<E>, Iterable<E>, SequencedCollection<E>, and Set<E>. The SequencedSet<E> type defines the following new method.

Table 3.2. New Methods in SequencedSet

Method Name and Return type	Description
SequencedSet<E> reversed()	Returns a reverse ordered view of the collection.

In the rearranged type hierarchy (Figure 3.3) the SortedSet interface extends the SequencedSet interface. The SortedSet interface is further extended by the NavigableSet interface. The only class that directly implements SequencedSet is LinkedHashSet.

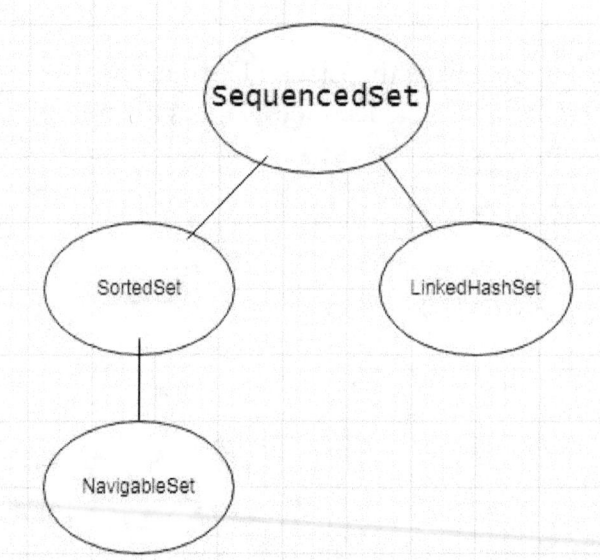

Figure 3.3. SequencedSet type hierarchy

The new SequencedMap type redefines the type hierarchy for Maps as shown in Figure 3.4. A SequencedMap has the following characteristics:

- The mappings (key-value pairs) in a sequenced map have a well-defined encounter order
- Supports operations at both ends
- Is reversible

The SequencedMap<E> type defines the following new methods; all the new methods except reversed() have a default implementation.

Table 3.3. New Methods in SequencedMap

Method Name and Return type	Description
default V putFirst(K k, V v)	Puts the given mapping as the first mapping. For repositioning support, makes the entry the first if already present in the map.
default V putLast(K k, V v)	Puts the given mapping as the last mapping. For repositioning support, makes the mapping the last if already present in the map.
SequencedMap<K,V> reversed()	Returns a reverse ordered view of the map. .
default SequencedSet<Map.Entry<K,V>> sequencedEntrySet()	Returns a SequencedSet view of this map's entrySet.
default SequencedSet<K> sequencedKeySet()	Returns a SequencedSet view of this map's keySet.
default SequencedCollection<V> sequencedValues()	Returns a SequencedCollection view of this map's values collection.

The SequencedMap<E> type promotes the following methods, which we discussed earlier, from the NavigableMap interface. All of these promoted methods provide default implementation, and the poll* methods are optional:

- default Map.Entry<K,V> firstEntry()
- default Map.Entry<K,V> lastEntry()
- default Map.Entry<K,V> pollFirstEntry()
- default Map.Entry<K,V> pollLastEntry()

What an "optional operation" means is that if a collection implementation does not support the operation the UnsupportedOperationException is thrown.

The re-arranged type hierarchy for Map is shown in Figure 3.5.

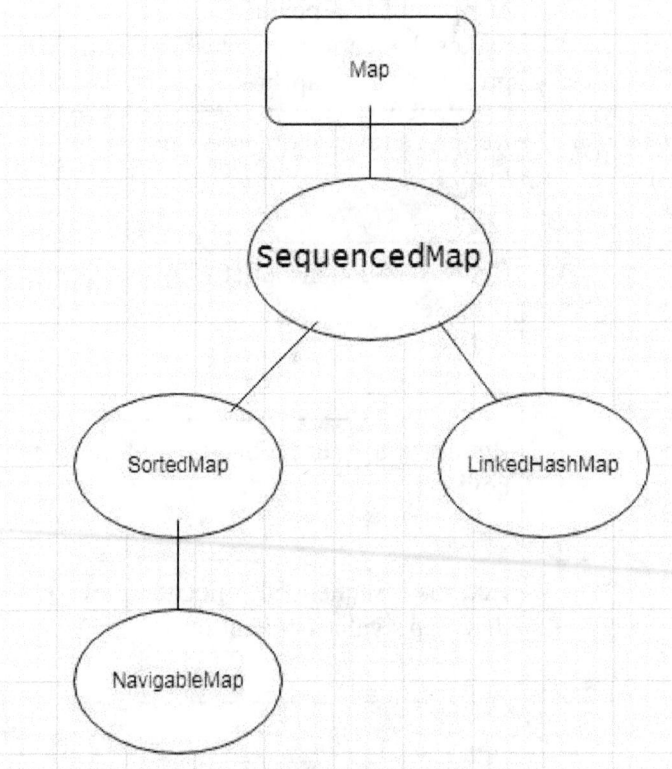

Figure 3.5. Re-arranged type hierarchy for Map

3.2 Summary

In this chapter we introduced what the sequenced collections language feature brings to the collections framework.

In subsequent chapters, we shall discuss the new, and existing, support for sequenced collections with examples.

4 Getting First and Last Elements

In this chapter, we will cover obtaining the first and last elements in a collection.

4.1 Before Sequenced Collections

Getting the first and last elements of a collection is very much feasible even before the sequenced collections feature in Java 21 although it may require some additional code inflection. As an example consider, the following sample application that gets and outputs the first and last elements of an ArrayList.

```java
import java.util.ArrayList;

public class Sample {

  public static void main(String[] args) {

    ArrayList < Integer > list = new ArrayList <
>();

    for (int i = 0; i < 5; i++) {

      list.add(i);
    }

    System.out.println("First element " +
list.get(0));
    System.out.println("Last element " +
list.get(list.size() - 1));
  }
}
```

The application makes use of get* methods to get the first and last methods with some added code inflection using list size to obtain the index of the last element,

The output from the application is as follows:

```
First element 0
Last element 4
```

4.2 With Sequenced Collections

Next, consider how the new API in Java 21 facilitates getting the first and last elements using the new API.

```java
import java.util.ArrayList;

public class Sample {

  public static void main(String[] args) {

    ArrayList < Integer > list = new ArrayList <
>();

    for (int i = 0; i < 5; i++) {

      list.add(i);
    }

    System.out.println("First element " +
list.getFirst());
    System.out.println("Last element " +
list.getLast());
  }
}
```

A simple call to the getFirst() and getLast() methods returns the first and last elements respectively:

```
First element 0
Last element 4
```

4.3 LinkedHashSet

A LinkedHashSet doesn't have any support for getting the first and last elements directly pre-Java 21.

4.3.1 Before Sequenced Collections

To demonstrate, create a LinkedHashSet<String> object and add some elements. To access the first/last elements convert the set to an array and subsequently get the first/last elements accessing the array at the first and last indices respectively.

```
size = set.size();

Object[] arr = (set.toArray());

System.out.println("First element " + arr[0]);
System.out.println("Last element " + arr[size - 1]);
```

The complete sample application is listed:

```
import java.util.LinkedHashSet;

import java.util.Iterator;


public class Sample {

   public static void main(String[] args) {

      int size = 0;

      LinkedHashSet < String > set = new
LinkedHashSet < >();

      for (int i = 0; i < 5; i++) {

        set.add("Element " + i);

      }
```

```
    size = set.size();

    Object[] arr = (set.toArray());

    System.out.println("First element " + arr[0]);

    System.out.println("Last element " + arr[size -
1]);

  }
}
```

Compile and run the Sample application with a Java version preceding 21 to get the first/last elements:

```
First element Element 0
Last element Element 4
```

4.3.2 With Sequenced Collections

Next, find how Java 21 makes it easier to get the first/last elements. A simple call to the new getFirst() and getLast() methods is all that is needed, as demonstrated in the sample application:

```
import java.util.LinkedHashSet;

public class Sample {

  public static void main(String[] args) {

    LinkedHashSet < String > set = new
LinkedHashSet < >();
    for (int i = 0; i < 5; i++) {

      set.add("Element " + i);
    }
    System.out.println("First element " +
set.getFirst());
```

```
    System.out.println("Last element " +
set.getLast());

    }
}
```

Compile and run the sample application with Java 21 to get the first/last elements:

```
First element Element 0
Last element Element 4
```

4.4 LinkedList

LinkedList already supports getFirst and getLast methods. The first and last elements may be obtained if a LinkedList is used as demonstrated in the sample application:

```
import java.util.LinkedHashSet;

import java.util.LinkedHashSet;

import java.util.LinkedList;


public class Sample {

    public static void main(String[] args) {

        LinkedHashSet < String > set = new
LinkedHashSet < >();

        for (int i = 0; i < 5; i++) {

            set.add("Element " + i);

        }
```

```
    LinkedList < String > list = new
LinkedList(set);

    System.out.println(list.getFirst());

    System.out.println(list.getLast());

  }
}
```

4.5 Summary

We started this chapter with an example of getting the first and last elements
with a Java version preceding Java 21. Subsequently, we demonstrated how
the new sequenced collections feature makes it easier in terms of method
calls.

In the next chapter, we explore how forward and reverse iteration the new
feature facilitates.

5. Forward and Reverse Iteration

Iteration is used to access elements of a collection in a sequential manner. In this chapter we explore forward and reverse iteration within a collection before, and with sequenced collections.

5.1 Forward Iteration

Forward iteration is already supported in the Collections framework before Java 21 introduced sequenced collections as a permanent language feature. To demonstrate, create a LinkedHashSet object, and add some elements to the collection. Obtain a forward iterator over the set and use a `while` loop to output the set's elements.

```
Iterator < String > iter = set.iterator();
while (iter.hasNext()) {
   System.out.println(iter.next());
}
```

The sample application to demonstrate forward iteration that is already supported pre-Java 21 is listed:

```
import java.util.LinkedHashSet;

import java.util.Iterator;


public class Sample {

   public static void main(String[] args) {

     LinkedHashSet < String > set = new
LinkedHashSet < >();

     for (int i = 0; i < 5; i++) {

       set.add("Element " + i);
```

```
    }

    Iterator < String > iter = set.iterator();

    while (iter.hasNext()) {

      System.out.println(iter.next());

    }

  }

}
```

The output from the application with Java 17 is as follows:

```
Element 0
Element 1
Element 2
Element 3
Element 4
```

5.2 Reverse Iteration

Reverse order iteration is already supported in a LinkedList using a descending iterator. To demonstrate, modify the sample application that we used for forward iteration, but this time create a LinkedList from the LinkedHashSet object and subsequently create a descending iterator as shown in the modified sample application:

```
import java.util.LinkedHashSet;

import java.util.Iterator;

import java.util.LinkedList;


public class Sample {

  public static void main(String[] args) {
```

```java
    LinkedHashSet < String > set = new
LinkedHashSet < >();

    for (int i = 0; i < 5; i++) {

        set.add("Element " + i);

    }

    LinkedList < String > list = new
LinkedList(set);

    Iterator < String > iter =
list.descendingIterator();

    while (iter.hasNext()) {

        System.out.println(iter.next());

    }

  }

}
```

Compile and run the application with Java 17 to get a reverse order listing of elements:

```
Element 4
Element 3
Element 2
Element 1
Element 0
```

5.3 Both Forward and Reverse Iteration

The ListIterator already supports forward/reverse iteration using the next() and previous() methods respectively. To demonstrate, create a Stack collection and add some elements to the stack. Subsequently, obtain a

ListIterator over the stack. First, iterate in the forward direction and output the stack's elements.

```java
while (iter.hasNext ()) {
   System.out.println (iter.next ());
}
```

Subsequently, iterate in the reverse direction to output a reversed view of the stack.

```java
while (iter.hasPrevious ()) {
   System.out.println (iter.previous ());
}
```

The sample application to demonstrate forward/reverse iteration using a ListIterator is listed:

```java
import java.util.ListIterator;

import java.util.Stack;


public class Sample {

   public static void main (String [] args) {

      Stack<Integer> stack = new Stack<>();

      stack.push (3);

      stack.push (5);

      stack.push (1);

      stack.push (2);

      stack.push (4);

      ListIterator<Integer> iter =
stack.listIterator ();
```

```
    // iterate forward

    while (iter.hasNext()) {

        System.out.println(iter.next());

    }

    // iterate backward

    while (iter.hasPrevious()) {

        System.out.println(iter.previous());

    }

    }

}
```

As the Stack is based on the Last-In-First-Out (LIFO) model, the stack's elements are output in the forward and reverse order when the sample application is run with Java 17.

```
3
5
1
2
4

4
2
1
5
3
```

5.4 Summary

In this chapter we explored forward and reverse iteration.
In the next chapter we discuss sequence reversal.

6. Reversed Sequence

Next, we discuss creating a reversed collection from an existing collection with the sequenced collections feature in Java 21. Java 17 does not support reversing a collection with a single method call.

6.1 Reversed LinkedHashSet

A reverse order collection can be made using the new reversed() method. First, create a LinkedHashSet object as before. Next, reverse the set collection as follows:

```
SequencedSet<String> seqSet=set.reversed();
```

Subsequently, obtain an iterator over the reversed collection and output its elements:

```
import java.util.LinkedHashSet;

import java.util.Iterator;

import java.util.SequencedSet;


public class Sample {

   public static void main(String[] args) {

   LinkedHashSet < String > set = new LinkedHashSet
< >();

      for (int i = 0; i < 5; i++) {

         set.add("Element " + i);

      }

      SequencedSet < String > seqSet =
set.reversed();
```

```
    Iterator < String > iter = seqSet.iterator();

  while (iter.hasNext()) {

      System.out.println(iter.next());

    }

  }

}
```

Compile and run the sample application with Java 21 to output the collection's elements in reverse order:

```
Element 4
Element 3
Element 2
Element 1
Element 0
```

6.2 Reversed Stack

Java 21 adds support for a reversed Stack using the reversed() method. A simple Iterator may be used to iterate over a reversed stack. To demonstrate, create a Stack and add some elements as before. Create a simple forward Iterator and output the stack's elements. Next, reverse the Stack as follows:

```
List<Integer> list=stack.reversed();
```

Obtain a simple Iterator over the reversed stack to output its elements. The sample application to demonstrate reversing a stack as as follows:

```
import java.util.Iterator;
import java.util.List;
import java.util.Stack;

public class Sample {
```

```java
public static void main(String[] args) {
    Stack<Integer> stack = new Stack<>();

    stack.push(3);
    stack.push(5);
    stack.push(1);
    stack.push(2);
    stack.push(4);

    Iterator<Integer> iter = stack.iterator();

    // iterate forward
    while (iter.hasNext()) {
        System.out.println(iter.next());
    }

    // reverse
    List<Integer> list = stack.reversed();
    iter = list.iterator();
    // iterate forward
    while (iter.hasNext()) {
        System.out.println(iter.next());
    }
  }
}
```

Compile and run the sample application with Java 21 to output a Stack's elements in forward and reverse order.

```
3
5
1
2
4

4
2
1
5
3
```

6.3 Reversed Sequenced Map

In this section we demonstrate the new reversed() method to reverse a LinkedHashMap and use the new SequencedMap type added in Java 21. As a Map has key-value pairs the sequence could be made at the map-entry level, the key-level or the value level. First, we shall reverse the sequence of the map entries. Create a LinkedHashMap<Integer,String> and add some map entries. Duplicate entries, if any, are not included in the map created. Reverse the map using the new reversed() method, and subsequently obtain an iterator over the reverse sequenced entry set.

```
SequencedMap<Integer,String>
reversedMap=map.reversed();
var itr=reversedMap.sequencedEntrySet().iterator();
```

Iterate over the elements in the reversed entry set and output the entries. The sample application is listed:

```
import java.util.Iterator;
import java.util.LinkedHashMap;
import java.util.SequencedMap;
public class Sample {
  public static void main(String[] args) {
    LinkedHashMap<Integer, String> map = new
LinkedHashMap<>();

    map.put(3,  "Third Value");
    map.put(4,  "Fourth Value");
    map.put(1,  "First Value");
    map.put(5,  "Fifth Value");
    map.put(2,  "Second Value");
    map.put(1,  "First Value");

    SequencedMap<Integer, String> reversedMap =
map.reversed();
    // var itr=reversedMap.entrySet().iterator();

    var itr =
reversedMap.sequencedEntrySet().iterator();
```

```
      while (itr.hasNext()) {
         System.out.println(itr.next());
      }
   }
}
```

Compile and run the Sample application with Java 21 with the following output:

```
2=Second Value
5=Fifth Value
1=First Value
4=Fourth Value
3=Third Value
```

Alternatively, a sequenced key set may be obtained using the sequencedKeySet() method in the SequencedMap type.

```
SequencedSet<Integer> seqSet=map.sequencedKeySet();
```

The sample application that outputs the sequenced key set is as follows:

```
import java.util.Iterator;
import java.util.LinkedHashMap;
import java.util.SequencedMap;
public class Sample {
   public static void main(String[] args) {
      LinkedHashMap<Integer, String> map = new
LinkedHashMap<>();

      map.put(3, "Third Value");
      map.put(4, "Fourth Value");
      map.put(1, "First Value");
      map.put(5, "Fifth Value");
      map.put(2, "Second Value");
      map.put(1, "First Value");

      SequencedMap<Integer, String> reversedMap =
map.reversed();
      // var itr=reversedMap.entrySet().iterator();
```

```
      var itr =
reversedMap.sequencedEntrySet().iterator();

    while (itr.hasNext()) {
      System.out.println(itr.next());
    }
  }
}
```

A sequenced key set is output when the sample application is compiled and run with Java 21.

```
3
4
1
5
2
```

6.4 Equivalent Methods in NavigableSet

Earlier it was mentioned that the reversed() method in SequencedCollection is essentially promoted from the NavigableSet::descendingSet method. What does that mean for the NavigableSet type? Well, it gets two methods that are equivalent: reversed and descendingSet(). The reversed() method that has origin in NavigableSet can be called in the NavigableSet. To demonstrate, create a TreeSet, which implements NavigableSet. Add some elements to the tree set. Call the reversed() method.

```
var navSet=set.reversed();
```

Obtain an iterator over the elements of the reversed set and output the elements. The Sample application that calls an equivalent method in NavigableSet is listed:

```
import java.util.Iterator;
import java.util.TreeSet;
public class Sample {
  public static void main(String[] args) {
```

```
TreeSet set = new TreeSet<>();

set.add(3);
set.add(4);
set.add(1);
set.add(5);
set.add(2);
set.add(1);
var navSet = set.reversed();
var itr = navSet.iterator();
while (itr.hasNext()) {
   System.out.println(itr.next());
   }
  }
}
```

Compile and run the sample application to output the elements in reversed order:

```
5
4
3
2
1
```

The implementation of reversed() in NavigableSet directly calls the descendingSet() method in the interface itself.

6.5 Summary

In this chapter we discussed reversing a sequenced collection using the new reversed() method.

7. Special Semantics

While adding a uniform support for sequenced access in the collections framework consideration is also made for special semantics in some of the collections API as needed.

7.1 LinkedHashSet

To be able to reposition elements of a Set the addFirst(E) and addLast(E) methods of the SequencedSet have special-case semantics for collections such as LinkedHashSet: When using these methods with a LinkedHashSet and if an element is already present in the set then it is moved to the appropriate first/last position, as a result reshuffling the collection. To demonstrate the repositioning feature create a LinkedHashSet<String> object and add some elements that are not in an ordered sequence.

```
LinkedHashSet<String> set = new LinkedHashSet<>();

set.add("Second Element");
set.add("Fifth Element");
set.add("First Element");
set.add("Fourth Element");
set.add("Third Element");
```

Next, reposition the misplaced elements by reading them as follows:

```
set.addFirst("First Element");
set.addLast("Fourth Element");
set.addLast("Fifth Element");
```

The complete sample application that outputs the elements of the unordered LinkedHashSet, and subsequently the elements of the ordered collection is as follows:

```
import java.util.Iterator;

import java.util.LinkedHashSet;

public class Sample {
```

```java
public static void main(String[] args) {

    LinkedHashSet<String> set = new
LinkedHashSet<>();

    set.add("Second Element");

    set.add("Fifth Element");

    set.add("First Element");

    set.add("Fourth Element");

    set.add("Third Element");

    Iterator<String> iter = set.iterator();

    while (iter.hasNext()) {

        System.out.println(iter.next());

    }

    set.addFirst("First Element");

    set.addLast("Fourth Element");

    set.addLast("Fifth Element");

    Iterator<String> iter2 = set.iterator();

    while (iter2.hasNext()) {

        System.out.println(iter2.next());

    }

}

}
```

Compile and run the application with Java 21 to get a repositioned-collection's output in addition to the original collection:

```
Second Element
Fifth Element
First Element
Fourth Element
Third Element

First Element
Second Element
Third Element
Fourth Element
Fifth Element
```

7.2 Stack Repositioning

While special semantics for repositioning a Stack's elements is not
supported in Java 21, a Stack's elements can be repositioned using the new
addFirst()/addLast() and removeFirst()/removeLast() elements. To
demonstrate, create a Stack and add some elements to it but not in an order
that you would want in an ordered collection.

```
Stack<Integer> stack = new Stack<>();
```

```
stack.push(3);
stack.push(5);
stack.push(1);
stack.push(2);
stack.push(4);
```

Next, reposition the stack's elements using the new add*/remove* methods
as follows:

```
stack.pop();
stack.addLast(3);
stack.addLast(4);
stack.addLast(5);
stack.removeFirst();
stack.removeFirst();
```

The sample application to reposition a Stack's elements is as follows:

```java
import java.util.Iterator;
import java.util.List;
import java.util.Stack;

public class Sample {
  public static void main(String[] args) {
    Stack<Integer> stack = new Stack<>();

    stack.push(3);
    stack.push(5);
    stack.push(1);
    stack.push(2);
    stack.push(4);

    Iterator<Integer> iter = stack.iterator();

    // iterate forward
    while (iter.hasNext()) {
      System.out.println(iter.next());
    }

    // reposition
    stack.pop();
    stack.addLast(3);
    stack.addLast(4);
    stack.addLast(5);
    stack.removeFirst();
    stack.removeFirst();
    iter = stack.iterator();
    // iterate forward
    while (iter.hasNext()) {
      System.out.println(iter.next());
    }
  }
}
```

Compile and run the sample application using Java 21 to output the elements of the repositioned Stack. The unordered stack and the ordered Stack output is as follows:

3
5
1
2
4

1
2
3
4
5

7.3 Special Semantics for LinkedHashMap

The new put*(K, V) methods have special-case semantics for maps such as the type LinkedHashMap. The new put*(K, V) methods reposition a map entry if it is already present in the map; both the Key and Value have to match for a new entry to be considered as the same as an existing entry. To demonstrate the special semantics, create a LinkedHashMap object and add some elements to it, perhaps not in an ordered manner.

```
map.put(3,"Third Value");
map.put(5,"Fifth Value");
map.put(4,"Fourth Value");
map.put(1,"First Value");
map.put(2,"Second Value");
```

Subsequently make some putFirst() and putLast() method calls to re-add some elements so as to reposition them.

```
map.putFirst(2,"Second Value");
map.putFirst(1,"First Value");
map.putLast(5,"Fifth Value");
```

The sample application to demonstrate repositioning is listed:

```
import java.util.Iterator;
```

```java
import java.util.LinkedHashMap;

import java.util.SequencedMap;

public class Sample {

  public static void main(String[] args) {

    LinkedHashMap<Integer, String> map = new
LinkedHashMap<>();

    map.put(3, "Third Value");

    map.put(5, "Fifth Value");

    map.put(4, "Fourth Value");

    map.put(1, "First Value");

    map.put(2, "Second Value");

    map.putFirst(2, "Second Value");

    map.putFirst(1, "First Value");

    map.putLast(5, "Fifth Value");

    var itr = map.sequencedEntrySet().iterator();

    while (itr.hasNext()) {

      System.out.println(itr.next());

    }

  }

}
```

Compile and run the application with Java 21. The output is ordered because elements get repositioned rather than getting added again.

```
1=First Value
```

```
2=Second Value
3=Third Value
4=Fourth Value
5=Fifth Value
```

7.4 Summary

In this chapter we discussed special semantics for a few of the collections framework types.

8. Unsupported and Optional Operations

We discussed using the explicit positioning methods such as addFirst()/addLast() in an earlier chapter. In this chapter we explore the limits of the explicit positioning methods among other unsupported operations on elements in a collection.

8.1 SortedSet and SortedMap

Because different collections make use of different types of comparators, not all new API for sequenced collections can be used for all types of collections. SortedSet and SortedMap determine the sequence of their elements by relative comparison. Therefore, explicit-positioning methods such as SortedSet::addFirst and SortedMap::putLast throw UnsupportedOperationException. .

To demonstrate, create a TreeSet, which implements SortedSet. Add some elements to the TreeSet. An iterator over the tree set may be obtained and its elements output. But, try calling the addFirst() method:

```
set.addFirst(0);
```

The sample application that makes a TreeSet::addFirst() method call is as follows:

```
import java.util.Iterator;

import java.util.TreeSet;

public class Sample {

  public static void main(String[] args) {

    TreeSet set = new TreeSet<>();

    set.add(3);

    set.add(4);
```

```java
        set.add(1);

        set.add(5);

        set.add(2);

        set.add(1);

        var itr = set.iterator();

        while (itr.hasNext()) {

            System.out.println(itr.next());

        }

        set.addFirst(0);

    }

}
```

Compile and run the sample application. Because a TreeSet implements SortedSet the elements are output sorted, but the UnsupportedOperationException gets generated:

```
1
2
3
4
5
Exception in thread "main"
java.lang.UnsupportedOperationException
        at
java.base/java.util.TreeSet.addFirst(TreeSet.java:4
76)
        at Sample.main(Sample.java:25)
```

8.2 LinkedHashMap

For maps such as LinkedHashMap, the explicit positioning methods have the additional effect of repositioning the entry if it is already present in the map. Duplicate mappings are removed in both the original entry set and sequenced entry set

To demonstrate, create a LinkedHashMap<Integer,String> object and add some elements to the collection. This time obtain a sequenced collection over its values.

```
SequencedCollection<String>
seqColl=map.sequencedValues();
```

Create an iterator over the values and output the sequenced values. However, if a call to the SequencedCollection<String>::addFirst() method is made, an exception is generated.

```
seqColl.addFirst("First Value");
```

The sample application to demonstrate obtaining sequenced values of a SequencedMap and subsequently calling the addFirst() method is listed:

```
import java.util.Iterator;
import java.util.LinkedHashMap;
import java.util.SequencedCollection;

public class Sample {
  public static void main(String[] args) {
    LinkedHashMap<Integer, String> map = new
LinkedHashMap<>();

    map.put(3, "Third Value");
    map.put(4, "Fourth Value");
    map.put(1, "First Value");
    map.put(5, "Fifth Value");
    map.put(2, "Second Value");
    map.put(1, "First Value");

    SequencedCollection<String> seqColl =
map.sequencedValues();

    var itr = seqColl.iterator();
```

```
    while (itr.hasNext()) {
       System.out.println(itr.next());
    }

    seqColl.addFirst("First Value"); // throws
exception
    }
}
```

Compile and run the sample application to output the sequenced values and the exception:

```
Third Value
Fourth Value
First Value
Fifth Value
Second Value
Exception in thread "main"
java.lang.UnsupportedOperationException
        at
java.base/java.util.LinkedHashMap$LinkedValues.addF
irst(LinkedHashMap
.java:838)
        at Sample.main(Sample.java:27)
```

8.3 Optional Operations

The new Sequenced Collection API marks several methods as "optional operation" so that an implementation does not have to implement these methods. A default implementation is provided for these optional operations.

8.4 Summary

In this chapter we discussed unsupported and optional operations. This chapter concludes this short book.

INDEX

www.ingramcontent.com/pod-product-compliance
Lightning Source LLC
LaVergne TN
LVHW051618050326
832903LV00033B/4554